BRANDING THE HEART

A GUIDE TO **DIGITAL ENGAGEMENT** FOR
NON-PROFIT ORGANIZATIONS

T I F F A N I   R O B I N S O N

http://JanCynCo.com

Table of Contents

FOREWORD

As digital platforms continue to evolve, Tiffani Robinson has created impactful strategies and methods that have taken international organizations to another level. With this book, she has poured out those strategies into a format that all of us can consume and benefit from. Whether it's ministries, churches, missions, outreach organizations, or any type of nonprofit, Tiffani has shown her expertise to be innovative, comprehensive, and useful. Watching her grow from an individual with an idea to an author with a platform has been a great opportunity and something that I will enjoy continuing to see flourish.

Jason Caston
Author
The iChurch Method

Dedicated To...

My Father, whose tenacity to protect and provide for his family instilled the desire to start this book...

My Mother, whose relentless dedication to her family and their wellbeing provided the motivation to continue writing this book...

and my Sister, whose dreams for a life well lived inspired me to finish this book.

I LOVE YOU WITH EVERYTHING!

—Tiff

Branding the Heart
By
Tiffani Robinson

Introduction

You have a passion. You have a vision. However, how do you translate the message of your vision or assignment into a language everyone will understand? What are the necessary tools? How do you use those tools to reach your target audience? No need to worry. By picking up this book, you have taken your first step towards the realization of your vision and carrying your message to the world.

Though you have passion or a purpose, neither of those is as important as the person behind them. Yes, a large group of people can support a particular goal. Nevertheless, it takes that one person—that singular personality—to ignite a fire in the hearts and minds of the individuals who join the cause. This is the main reason behind the title, *Branding the Heart*.

No one can do exactly what you do the way you do it. There are 7 billion people on the planet. Out of that enormous number, hundreds of thousands of people have the same idea as you do. They also have the same zeal and fervency for the particular subject or cause that has captured your attention. What, then, differentiates you from them? It is your heart. It is your individuality. It is your uniqueness that will draw people in. Therefore, it is necessary for people to see *you*!

The purpose of *Branding The Heart* is to quickly and efficiently equip you with the basics you will need in order for your targeted audience to hear your message, respond to it with their support, and see your heart throughout the entire process. There is a developing science to Social Media. Whether you are soliciting financial donations, garnering awareness, or requesting people to unite with you in taking action, the galvanizing force people will follow in everything you do is *you*. I will show you how to use this "science" to further your cause.

I want this to not only be a learning experience, but an enjoyable one! At first glance, the task of implementing a digital engagement plan into your marketing strategy can be daunting. Because of the nature of this challenge, I want to assist you in the best ways possible. Therefore, I will use the *hashtag,* #PulseCheck, to provide you with some helpful tactics that will keep you on "beat" with the branding essence of your online goal. From learning and knowing your target audience, all the way to implementing and tailoring your plan for continued success, this handy guide will assist you throughout your online life.

So, let's get started. Welcome to *Branding The Heart*.

Tiffani

Chapter 1

The Story

You woke up one day with an idea. After seeing a problem, witnessing an event or hearing of some calamity, you decided something should be done. Then, your idea was conceptualized, taking a specific shape in your mind that hammered home the necessity of action. Congratulations! You have, officially, become the vehicle through which this awesome idea and concept of yours will be born into the world.

It's the start of a new season, and you realize the importance of relevancy pertaining to your digital strategies. When looking forward and planning, it's always beneficial to reflect on the past. To somehow address that which has moved us, correct that which has frustrated us, or remember that which has forever changed us. This is reflection in its truest form. This is the birth of storytelling. In the marketing field, I have seen the rapid advancement of this process with varied results, sometimes with unproductive redundancy and little improvement. I blame this confusion on agencies' desires for a competitive edge rather than directing their efforts inward to evolving their identity. You see, no one foresees the future; they only predict what it will be based off of previous knowledge. With this knowledge, these projections are best executed through relevant, developed approaches that engage and move your following.

So, I'd like to ask you a few questions: What is so special about your idea? How is your concept drastically different from someone else with an identical objective?

The difference is your **story**.

Quite simply, your story is what you want to say, how you will convey it, and the "why" behind it all. It is the detailing of how you arrived at the importance of the subject at hand and the proposed response that will bring about a desired end. Your story will use the Internet to convey your persona into social mediums. Your story is the connective tissue between the initial cause and the required action. It is the heart of your entire campaign. It, therefore, must be emotionally compelling.

Say, for instance, you desire to bring awareness to a particular issue. Your story, then, would answer the questions, "What is the issue?" And, "Why is it so important?" Take a brief look at the recent upsurge of human trafficking. Though this problem has existed for hundreds of years, it, again, recently caught the world's attention as a result of news outlets reporting the abduction of over two hundred women in Nigeria. Yes, it is an atrocity. Yes, it must be dealt with. But, *why* is it so important to you? More importantly, why should people donate specifically to you and follow your directions for addressing the plight of the thousands of people abducted every year?

These questions present you with the invaluable opportunity to persuade your audience to get on board with your plan. So, tell your story.

Let's say you wish to raise awareness of cultural inequality. This equality could be financial, racial, gender-based or even centered in social classes. At least one of these examples has taken place on each of the six continents man overwhelmingly inhabits. Stories of inequality take over the news every now and then, so it is best to discover how to really drive home your story without it needing the assistance of mainstream media. Take, for instance, the racial inequality experienced by many in Ferguson, Missouri and abuse of police powers in New York City. Hundreds of people were affected after initial incidents. However, if your story discloses that you attached yourself to this problem as a result of you or a family member *directly* being a victim of any kind of inequality, particularly of the sort in Ferguson and New York, that one detail adds an extra layer of complexity and personal proximity through which other people will be drawn into your campaign to raise awareness.

It is there you are able to delve into greater detail. Though giving a detailed account of the type of inequality experienced and the emotions felt and expressed during the ordeal, the investigation into the situation and its results might seem off-putting to some. These elements of your story are the very things that tug at the strings of people's hearts. Not only have you succeeded at capturing your audience's attention, you have involved their emotions simply by giving nothing more than a narrative.

Your story develops a **trust factor** between your organization and the masses. Your followers—and we are not just talking about Social Media followers, though they are included—will see you as an authority in the field of your subject. The more they trust you, the more they listen to the voice of your online persona. The more they listen, the more they follow. The more they follow, the more apt they are to contribute to your cause, participate in your demonstrations, or pass along your message and increase awareness.

This trust factor, then, must allow for some aspect of your uniqueness to be used to open a door for your following to share their own stories.

If your story provides an avenue through which you begin a relationship with your followers, and your followers find something in your story that speaks directly to them, then your story must be a mirror in which others see themselves—a method through which they are able to tell their own stories! In essence, your story provides the perfect setup for a mutually beneficial relationship.

Now, if you remember correctly, I mentioned that there is a minute difference between your story and that of someone else. However, for your brand to stand up and call attention to a specific issue and gather a following, that following must have found some similarity in your uniqueness with which they have been touched. No two people's stories are exactly alike because the perception and lenses through which both people see life and their experiences are different. How, then, does this provide an opportunity for both the followers and brand to grow? This can be summed up in one word—*symbiosis*.

Allow me to explain.

Your brand is meant to call attention to something—a lack of services, a human rights violation, a sickness and its need for a cure. Whatever the reason, your brand has become a voice for the voiceless. There are issues all over this planet that have not been addressed. However, have you noticed how tons of people speak up after that one whistleblower gathers the courage to clear their throat, speak about an issue, and bring awareness where there was none previously? You have seen it in scandals in Hollywood all the way to the White House. Something happens, and it goes unchecked for whatever period of time. As a result, others are affected. Then, someone comes forward and says something. That one person brave enough to say something acts as a singular voice for the thousands—if not millions—of people who have been affected in some way by the same or similar situation. The same thing happens with your brand.

Yes, your story is different. Yes, the variables in your story are different from those in someone else's. Nevertheless, others look to you and your brand to be and do the very thing they can't—**be a conduit** *through which others can tell their own stories*! Once you understand this, a symbiotic relationship forms between you and your followers. But, what is *symbiosis*?

Symbiosis—interaction between two different organisms living in close physical association, typically to the advantage of both.

Now, we all know that most of us are not living right next to each other or in the same house, let alone the same neighborhood. However, one of the many wonderful things about the Internet is its ability to bring together people from all around the world. We have virtual friends, virtual hangouts, and virtual neighborhoods all because of the interconnectivity we have through the world wide web. This global community made possible by the Internet allows each of us to benefit from merely interacting with one another.

Imagine that your brand's website is up and running, and you have some wonderful web traffic happening. You take a look at your analytics (we will discuss "analytics" later in the book) and notice some similarities that permeate your entire online audience. As you delve deeper into your research and participate even more in the online conversation between your brand and its followers, you see that people have become advocates for your brand because they have experienced the very thing to which your brand is calling attention. These people have become an online army that supports your initiatives and spreads the message and story of your brand.

Do you see what happened in that scenario?

The very story they told to others is their own, but it all leads back to the story you've told. Both of you have benefited through your virtual relationship. Your brand's notoriety and awareness has increased because of the actions of your followers, while your followers got to experience the gift of telling someone else their own story. Your brand was the pipeline that carried someone else's story to a completely different destination from which your brand will likely gain even more followers!

That, my friends, is an online symbiotic relationship!

Your brand's story must be reinforced at all points of contact within your marketing components. From the name of your cause, to the message you are delivering, and to the follow-up calls, emails, tweets or posts, your people must remember why they have linked themselves to you and your brand. The moment people forget why they are working with you, investing time into communicating with you, or financially contributing to your cause, you lose them as a valuable resource. This is why it is necessary for you to keep in mind that your cause adds value to not only your life, but the lives of your followers. When a follower believes they are a part of your brand, they begin to see themselves and what they do as an investment. As an investment, they will likely remain with you for the long haul simply because they see within your brand a reward or return on their investment.

The word, *brand*, means "to burn." In essence, this is what companies do to our brains with the massive advertising tactics they use. It can become an overwhelming experience to constantly and consistently get hammered with images of a brand that sometimes lack any kind of real substance behind their campaigns. Companies with the most successful promotions do not excessively push or coerce consumers. They build relationships with their customers. Most often, these relationships are life-long and built through accessibility, approach, and awareness.

Take a look at the following examples.

Whole Foods

Whole Foods has the ability to successfully adapt and alter their marketing approaches to each social network while maintaining engaging campaigns. This is also exercised through their individualized approach for each store location on the web. Each Whole Foods store has their own Social Media page that personalizes the user experience in the online community. Users aren't faced with the task to navigate through the web to find information related to their specific need (region) due to the Whole Foods

Central Hub that links to the sub pages (other stores). Whole Foods also has a distribution schedule for content in place of which the user gains a familiarity and begins setting expectations. Because of this, the user becomes a loyal customer.

Questions to consider…

- What do I wish to convey? Am I aiming to bring awareness to a specific matter, or am I combatting a problem that requires financial contributions? Both?
- Is my topic notable, or worthy of attention and a response?
- Does this topic have longevity, or is it a situation that will be resolved in the next few days? In other words, how far will it go?
- Can my cause attain a level of notoriety? Can it retain followers? Does it have the power to maintain itself over time?

Taking your story into account, you must be able to provide strong answers to these questions, and the stronger the better.

In order to help you better understand the necessity and power of a story, we are going to examine one of my favorite online advocacy websites: www.FallingWhistles.com.

Case Study 1.1: Falling Whistles

Have you ever found yourself completely consumed by a book that you couldn't put it down? The same method in captivating a reader should transpire with each story for your online presence. A great cause to follow in the building and execution of strategies for storytelling is **Falling Whistles.**

When he arrived back on U.S. soil, he wanted to tell everyone about what he had seen: the deadliest war of our time still unfolding - unnoticed and unchallenged. But war isn't so easily brought up in casual conversation. Then a friend Marcus gave him a unique gift: a whistle on a chain. Worn around his neck, it sparked interest everywhere he went.

That's when they realized: Their weapon could be our voice.

They began selling whistles out of their pockets, asking everyone they met to be a whistleblower for peace. A young man David then took a box of whistles and hitchhiked from Austin, Texas to New York City.

Along the way he stopped in living rooms and coffee shops with a simple message: "We don't have all the answers, but we won't be quiet while millions lose their lives." Three college students were inspired by him and rode their bikes from Florida to California carrying whistles in their satchels. One by one, person by person, the message began to spread.

(Falling Whistles' story & visuals)

The very first encounter the visitor has on the Falling Whistles page is a beautifully narrated video accompanied by compelling visuals that bring the story to life. By the conclusion of the video, the visitor is left with the overwhelming sensation to take action. It is there they are presented with the opportunity to join the cause by making an average $35+ purchase of an item directly associated with the cause. This provides an instant camaraderie with an entire movement. This is digital engagement through storytelling at its finest.

Original

$50.00

STORY
In the Winter of 2008, a young man walked into the Democratic Republic of Congo. Five escaped child-soldiers told him that boys, too small to carry a gun, were being sent to the front lines, armed with only a whistle. Since that day, a coalition of young and old, rich and poor, have fought - side by side - toward a dream most would call impossible. PEACE in CONGO *Make their weapon* YOUR voice
Be a WHISTLEBLOWER *for* PEACE

ORIGINAL
The Original Whistle is our first and most popular whistle. It's a chrome whistle and hangs on a aluminum ball-chain. The shininess of The Original Whistle gives it a classic and versatile look that goes with just about everything.
SIZE: 8 x 1 cm
Chain: 84 cm

PACKAGE
We are genuinely proud of our new packaging. The paper is made out of unbleached and recycled material and it's held together by a waxed cotton thread with a Falling Whistles seal. The inside holds the story that we are still writing to this day, together, with you.

DELIVERY AND SHIPPING
All products ship from Sweden. Shipping to the rest of Europe and to USA usually takes 4-7 working days. Other international shipping could take a some additional days.
International shipping is free, but if you're looking to contribute more you can always choose to cover the shipping cost at the end of the check-out process.

(Falling Whistles' online store)

Once you have instilled that seed of empathy through your storytelling, the visuals that surround the content will begin to water and grow inside the viewer. It is at the online store of Falling Whistles that the flower of advocacy begins to bloom. Though it is simplistic in nature, the creators provide a definitive goal that carries the visitor from curiosity to purpose. Within the description of each piece, they are continually stamping the phrase, *"Be a whistleblower for peace,"* at the end, thereby compelling the viewer to not just become a part of a purpose, but own it and share.

--

We have to accept that we are in the midst of more informed, insightful consumers that have tools readily available to them at the tip of their fingers. To merely stay in a traditional phase and not take the risk of accepting new and innovative methods in your brand strategy would be an injustice to your followers and a detriment to your progression. This is where you differentiate who you are in your market. So, I challenge you. In the words of my favorite cartoon character, Miss Frizzle, "Take chances, make mistakes, and get messy." Your customers will love you for it.

#PulseCheck: A great tool to utilize for storytelling is SnapChat. SnapChat is a video and photo messaging app that allows users to add text and drawings to their post and send them to a controlled list of recipients or the general public. Be mindful, however, your "snaps" only last a designated time and disappear once that time has elapsed. This makes the storyteller very mindful of the purpose of the post, as well as the content.

Chapter 2

Strategy

Congratulations on solidifying your story! I am absolutely sure your story is emotionally engaging and invites people to join your cause or even donate to your mission. Though you have a killer story, you are not quite ready to make your debut to the world yet. There are several additional steps you must take before you can successfully introduce your brand to the masses. As a result, you do not simply take your story and upload it to the myriad amount of social networks and hope to gain some attention. No. You examine your story, realizing there is a certain group of people you are targeting. Based on your story and targeted audience, your next course of action is to develop a *strategy*. Shot-gunning your story across all social mediums will produce nothing but headaches, frustration and fits of you loudly questioning the validity of your efforts while you rock back and forth in a corner. This is your one shot to leave a mark on the digital stratosphere and you don't want to use this opportunity to shoot into a deep abyss of ambiguity. Be clear, direct and meticulous. Similar to chess, you are always playing moves far ahead of your current state.

This strategy will determine the medium you will use, be it Facebook, Tumblr, Twitter, Google+, Vimeo, Vine or YouTube. A marketing company would house their strategy in a creative brief. If you are doing this alone, this strategy provides a roadmap to which you will always refer back.

Imagine a female in her early to mid twenties happening upon someone's story that originally targeted males in their early thirties. As you can easily guess, that story would not make much of an impact on that young lady. However, what if she were to stumble upon a blog about female millennials in the corporate environment? What if she discovered this blog was written by a woman in her same age range? Not only is this young lady more apt to regularly visit and read the blog, she will likely share it on her personal Facebook page, tweet about it and tell her friends. Do you see what happened? All this young lady did was respond to something that was specifically geared to her. The people in your audience need to feel like you are talking directly to them. Therefore, it is best to model your targeted audience on *you*! The reason for this is that your story affected you enough to cause you to take action. If it was that effective with you, it stands to reason that it would similarly affect others like you.

Crafting the strategy for your story is of utmost importance. For, what difference does it make to have a wonderful story that would move the hearts of millions to join your cause if those same millions of people never see your story? So, how does your brand gain traction on the internet? First, let us take a look at your targeted audience. In order to do this, you must have a persona in mind. The persona is the ideal person you are trying to reach. Your strategy's aim is completely built around that one person. Why? Simple. To gain the attention of one individual who matches the persona of who would respond to your story is to gain the attention of thousands of others just like them. Remember the 7 billion people mentioned earlier? Just like there are thousands of people with similar stories as you, there are thousands of others who will respond just like the one individual matching your targeted persona. Recall that it is best to model that persona on you.

An excellent example to note when it comes to reaching and sounding like your targeted persona is portrayed in an ingenious advertisement campaign employed by Discover Card. In a slew of their commercials, you will notice two characters. One of those characters is the Discover Card customer service representative, and the other is a customer who has phoned in with a specific question. Look closely at the two characters and you will see that they are similarly styled. Their hair is alike. Their style of dress is comparable. Even their communication styles are a spot on match! Plus, both of them will either acknowledge or laugh at a point that no one else would consider worthy of attention. That is the hook. The two characters look and sound like each other and respond similarly to the same things. To hammer the point home, Discover Card closes out the commercial spots with their campaign's slogan: "*We treat you like YOU'D treat you!*"

It is perfect! And, you can attain that same perfection just by studying your targeted persona.

Keep this persona in your mind throughout the entire process. Your story, your strategy, your brand will continuously speak to that "person". Let us take a look at our previous example—the female millennial we met a few moments ago. Her name is Jennifer. Jennifer is a single twenty-four-year-old who just landed an entry position in her field of collegiate study. She has her own place, makes a decent salary and rents an apartment in a trendy area of her city. Jennifer eats right and works out when she can. When she's not at work or working out, Jennifer is traveling and hanging with her family and friends. Right now, as you read, there is a more detailed picture of Jennifer forming in your mind. The more details I give you, the more intricate the picture becomes and the more you get to know Jennifer. Why are all these specifics and "facts" important about this fictitious Jennifer? They are important because they determine Jennifer's online habits, such as the websites she visits, her posting frequency and how often she checks her social media feeds. That information helps you determine the details in your strategy, such as when you are posting, the usage of keywords and whether you will use Twitter instead of Facebook or other sites. Again, if there is one Jennifer, there are thousands of women just like her, and those thousands are potential followers or contributors. We want to speak to all of the "Jennifer's" in the world and their interests.

Now that you have a small outline of Jennifer, it is necessary to delve just a little deeper into detail about her. Though you possess some general knowledge about her, there is far more about Jennifer, and women like her, that you need to know in order to craft an effective strategy. This is because each Jennifer can be distinctly different from the next when you take into account the regions you are targeting, education level, history of the area and myriad other facets. For instance, you would not communicate with Jennifer in the upper west side of Manhattan the same way you would communicate with Jennifer in South Central Los Angeles. Their regions are completely different, as well as the surrounding cultures and styles of speech. Now, do not be afraid.

Though knowing every minute detail about your targeted persona can be helpful, it is not necessary to get bogged down in minutia. Your story will get out there and reach the right people.

The Theory of Homophily

I want to give you a bit of science behind the old phrase, "Birds of a feather flock together." After all, in various ways, the advent and phenomenon of Social Media is based on the application of that phrase. This old adage can be summed up in one word: *Homophily.* This word is literally translated to mean "love of the same." It describes the human, wonderful tendency of individuals to associate and bond with those who are similar to them in some way.

Imagine meeting someone for the first time. After getting through the awkward small talk, you begin to discover some things about one another. If you spend enough time with that person over a series of days, weeks, months, and years, you even form a friendship. How did that friendship form? In you learning about each other, you found out that you and the other person shared some similarities. Those similarities lead to other similarities. After a time, you guys realized you had more similarities than you had differences. Now, here comes the kicker.

Your new friend has brought someone else into this wonderful relationship you two share. You have never met the third individual. However, upon your friend introducing the "stranger", you are told that the similarities you two share are also shared by the stranger. You spend a few hours, days, or weeks with the stranger all to discover that the stranger is not a stranger at all. They are another manifestation of a different aspect of you. You and the stranger become friends. This process continues for however long with you seeing that your circle of friends and associates has grown exponentially over a small amount of time.

Just as this process occurs in your day to day life, it occurs at a much faster rate online. I can prove it to you. Have you noticed the column on the right side of your computer screen when you log on to Facebook? Not only do you see a series of pages you are invited to like; you will notice people who are connected to your friends and to the pages you have already liked.

Most of the time, you will see people you know that have not yet become your friend. That connection—that invisible binding string that ties you to other individuals is defined as homophily. It is this phenomenon that causes your brand's notoriety to increase. If your friends, Michael and Lisa, are connected to your brand's page, you can guess with some aspect of certainty that some of their friends will become your followers when Michael and Lisa become noncommissioned advocates of your brand and spread the news. You are connected to Michael and Lisa. Michael and Lisa are connected to their friends. Their friends, therefore, bring their friends...and so on, and so on.

The context of how messages are communicated will always supersede the messages content simply because humans relate to one another through applicable context and not just information. When we release information into the world, we typically follow a model, such as the following:

Audience > Genomes > Individuals

Our brands have a collection of followers that we call our audience. However, when we take a closer look at our audiences, we see that they have smaller groups within the mass assembly of individuals. These smaller groups share connections with one another that they do not necessarily share with other members of the larger group. As we focus our microscope a bit more to see even smaller organisms, we eventually arrive at the **individual** level. We want to reach each individual. Unfortunately, we do not always directly affect or grab everyone. Nevertheless, there is a large probability that we will when we engage in using our followers' networks (**genomes**) to broaden and strengthen the web of our brand's followers. So, instead of working from a macroscopic scale on the audience level, we begin laying the foundations of our brand's network on the microscopic scale of the individual we desire to reach. This is why it is imperative that you have a *persona* in mind. The formula, then, looks like this:

Individual > Genomes (Networks) > Audience

As you can see, by reaching one individual, their network can potentially yield hundreds and thousands of followers for your brand. By implementing the Theory of Homophily, you are, in essence, placing the power of brand awareness in the hands of the people you are trying to reach. Humans are creatures of habit and familiarity. Provide them with the information—no matter if it is good or bad—and they will immediately inform their network (genomes) of friends and like-minded individuals.

"Birds of a feather flock together." That statement is never more true than in Social Media. This is exactly why you see the same people on your Facebook timeline. That group of people within your network is the most relevant to your profile.

I implore you: Use homophily to your brand's benefit!

Though your persona does drive your strategy, you must also take into account the amount and type of information you wish to disclose. That amount will help determine which online tool you will use. For instance, if blogging is your desire, Tumblr or Medium might be your best bet. Are you looking for smaller, more frequent posts? Then a microblogging site, like Twitter, could accommodate you very well. If you wish to go the multimedia route, Vimeo, YouTube, Vine or Instagram could provide you with what you need. However, like Facebook's more generous character-count limit and Twitter's 140 character-count limit, multimedia sites require you to examine the amount of information you wish to expose. Vine typically allows only six-second videos. Instagram allows for fifteen seconds, while Vimeo and YouTube allow you to post videos of any length.

Now, it is time to think about how you will implement your strategy. Will you Blog, Microblog, or use Multimedia. I am not one for limits, so you can imagine my answer being to use all three...*as long as they fit your persona*. Let's discuss our options.

Blogging

At some point in time, you have visited a blog site and read a blog. We all have. "Blog" is a shortened version of the word, "Weblog." It simply became easier to say in a shortened fashion. Google tells us that a blog is a regularly updated website or web page that is typically run by an individual or small group. It is written in an informal or conversational style. As mentioned above, Facebook, Tumblr, and Twitter are types of blogs. However, those like Instagram, Vimeo, YouTube, and Vine are called "vlogs"—shortened form of "Video log'.

Facebook and Tumblr provide an inexhaustible amount of space in which you can post your thoughts. At first, Facebook limited its users to a 420 character-count in order to keep posts brief. Facebook has removed that limit, allowing you to post blog entries of any length. Nevertheless, just because Facebook and Tumblr do not have limits does not mean you should write anthologies that take decades to read. A long blog post, regardless of where it is, is the first excuse a follower or potential follower will use in the reasoning behind no longer following you or giving you their attention. Keep your blogs as short as possible while filling them with pertinent substance.

Microblog

Twitter is the quintessential microblogging site. A microblog is the same as a blog, but on a much smaller scale. Remember the abolished 420 character-count on Facebook? Well, Twitter still has a limit. It is 140 characters. See? Microblogging is just blogging on a smaller scale. Though it is smaller, there is no discounting the option of microblogging. Twitter has added some wonderful features to their infrastructure that almost makes microblogging a necessity to any brand's strategy. However, the main purpose for microblogging is to allow for smaller, spare-of-the-moment posts that really do not need a specific target. They are meant to be posted and released to any and all who would read or hear them. Even though they have a blitzkrieg nature to them, even your microblogs can be targeted with the correct keywords and hashtags, but more on those later.

Multimedia

Sometimes, a simple text post will not do. There is a reason for the saying, "A picture is worth a thousand words." I am in total agreement with that. I will also say that a video is worth a million pictures. I guarantee you that a properly created photo or video will receive, at the very least, five times more notoriety and views than a normal text update or blog entry. Why is that? It is simple. The brain can process an image seen for only 13 milliseconds, proving that our minds work according to concepts instead of just language. You can get far more information across to your audience at a much more rapid pace than you can with text. This is why you are seeing Facebook timelines, Twitter feeds, and Instagram feeds with an overwhelming population of photos and videos. Though I can give you all the information you can handle to prove my point, I will ask you a simple question: Would you like to read a four-page article about your brand, or see a video and slew of photos? Do you see my point, now?

Currently, the best social multimedia sites or apps are Instagram, Vine, YouTube, and Vimeo. Instagram and Vine can be considered microvlogs, staying within a certain time-limit for videos while allowing for photos. YouTube and Vimeo do not have limits on the length of videos that you can post. However, remember that the average person has a limit on how long they will stare at their smartphones, tablets, computer screens, and television sets. So, keep your multimedia posts as brief as possible while making them irresistible to watch.

Having a proper balance between blogs, microblogs, and multimedia is integral to the success of the implementation of your strategy because you will be communicating with your followers while looking to attract new followers. Everyone has a favorite way of receiving information. Because we all are different, it would behoove you to use as wide a net as possible to try to catch all of the followers that come your way.

Search Engine Optimization

But, what about people who are trying to find you through a random search on Google or another search engine? How do you ensure that you will be found when that person types a certain word in the search box? Enter the world of **Search Engine Optimization.** Now, do not be intimidated by those three words. Trust me. Once you know what **SEO** (search engine optimization) is, your nervousness will disappear.

Search Engine Optimization is a fancy way of describing the process of affecting the visibility of your website or page in a search engine's results. Do a Google search of your favorite thing—anything, it does not matter. The results that Google returns to you are formatted in a series of pages. You can see the number of pages by scrolling to the bottom and seeing the line of numbers bracketed by arrows that point to the left and right. Google can return search results from one page to hundreds of pages. Each of those results has something to do with your initial search in some shape, form, or fashion. Now, how many times have you gone past the first page of results when looking for what you need? How about the second? Third? Fifth? Ninth? Therein lies the necessity for search engine optimization.

You want—scratch that—you *need* to be on the first page, preferably in the top five returned results. Why? Typically, the higher and earlier you are on the search results page, the more visitors you will receive from the search engine's users.

Google, like every other search engine, uses their own algorithms to move through the internet and return to you all that pertains to your initial search. Their algorithm takes into account frequency and number of visits to sites, location, photos and videos, and a plethora of other variables to ensure that what you see on screen is a viable answer to your question or search. The more viable the answer, the higher and earlier it is in the results. Hence, your desire to be high on the first page. In order to be high and early in the returned search results, a site must have the proper keywords built into their site during its construction. The same goes for your brand's site. Your keywords should include the brand's name, focus, and just about anything that will cause a search engine to return even the most minute aspect of your brand to a user who is looking for something.

Now that we have discussed the various types of blogs and how to ensure your brand has a high visibility rate and ranks highly in the search results, it is time you take all of this into account with the amount of information your strategy requires you to share.

Upon answering the question of the amount of information you are going to unleash, it will behoove you to set a posting schedule. Certain groups of people, like those similar to your persona, are online at particular times. Know these high traffic times! They are visiting specific sites, posting about distinct issues and responding accordingly all out of a habit based on their availability time. An elderly gentleman might not be up at eleven at night, while a college student is not only up, but actively answering posts. Both sets of individuals have unique time periods in which they respond to what they see on the net. This means that you have to schedule your posting at the right time in order to make sure your content is in the top several posts of their feed. Scheduled post is not only beneficial in who you reach but it also time and cost efficient. By scheduling posts in advance you save on time and therefore the manpower used as opposed to a set, inflexible time you would adhere to otherwise. A good strategy knows its persona and tailors everything around that group, including its schedule.

As you implement your strategy, it is only right that you know exactly how effective it is. In comes the necessary usage of analytical tools. Yes, you can see how many people have "liked" a post on Facebook, or even see how many people "Favorited" and "Retweeted" one of your Tweets. However, that basic level of information is far from conclusive when it comes to you needing to know how many times your content has been viewed, who viewed it and when. You are looking to see if your content has gained online traction. The best way to see that is not only by how many people have joined your cause or donated, but also by viewing the volume of traffic to your site, blog or multimedia content. This gives you an accurate picture of how many "eyes" have landed on your information.

Say you have instituted your plan, and things have been going swimmingly for the past few weeks. Donations are up. You have gotten a wonderful response from people backing you and your cause. Comments have come in. Positive feedback abounds. You feel satisfied with your current results. One day, however, I walk into your establishment and set up a few analytical tools on your blog or site. After several days of monitoring, I come back to you and walk you through my discoveries. My findings say that, though you have plenty of responses from how you have employed your plan, you can increase those same responses by 175% simply by adjusting your posting schedule of new content from early morning to mid afternoon. This information is based on your targeted audience, or persona, viewing your content and responding to it during their lunch break.

Analytics can tell you all this information and more, giving you just about everything you need to help you adjust your schedule and amend any content to not only keep the traffic you have, but also increase it! There are plenty of Analytics tools you can purchase. Some are even free, like Google Analytics! There are others, of course: 33Across, Brandwatch, Hootsuite, Buffer, LocalResponse, Moz Analytics and SproutSocial. Each of them offers something different to their customers, based on the scope and specificity of the information required. All you must do is choose the company that best fits your goals and necessities.

So, get started on examining the persona you desire to reach. Take a long look at the amount of material you want to release, and start seeing which online tools best fit your goals. Completing these steps will help you further develop your strategy and your schedule. To help you with developing your strategy, examine with me our next case study—Elite Daily.

Case Study 2.1: Elite Daily

When identifying, acquiring, and maintaining a targeted demographic, one of the leaders ahead of the content realm is *Elite Daily*. *Elite Daily* is an online internet news media company *specifically* geared for Millennials. There is no mistake who Elite Daily wants to connect with and what they want to convey with their continual push of pointed content. As the self-proclaimed "voice of the generation-y", their website and social mediums are full of advice columns, articles on light-hearted viral stories that attracts and retains consistent viewership from the 20-something, romantic, wanderlust, post grad entrepreneurial persona. What makes the connection so poignant is that the viewer is represented by the writer. The exact person who is writing the content is in essence the one who is reading it—their peers. This is imperative when trying to relate any online engagement to a desired audience.

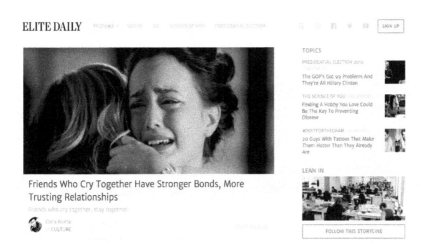

I can't stress the importance of strategy. One of the earliest examples most of us have experienced with strategy is Battleship. You stand as Commander for a fleet of naval ships varying in shapes and through "guestimation" place you ships along a grid in attempt to camouflage them from attacks. Then we take our pegs and place them on the upper tier of the board game to attack the opponent. Now whether you place the pegs sporadically or meticulously in an organized manner you have executed a strategy. It isn't until you finally hit a ship that you place more pegs around the area of the initial attack. You begin to have a more developed awareness of where that ship might be on the other side of the partition. The same principles should be implemented in your efforts at targeting and connecting with your desired audience. Once you reach them take an effort to learn them, restructure and perfect that strategy.... then repeat! When you evolve effectively you grow exponentially.

#PulseCheck: One of the tools you can utilize to bring your persona to life is Person [http://personapp.io/]. This app allows you to build a persona that embodies the desired demographic you seek to reach in your digital engagement efforts. This is the framework for the foundation of your strategy.

Chapter 3

Your Content

You have your story, and I know it's wonderful, emotional and impactful. You have developed your strategy, ironing out its details based upon the persona you are attempting to reach. You have nailed down the times you are going to post and the social media platforms you will use. By now, you have even chosen the mediums you will employ in order to convey your message. You have come quite a long way since we began this journey in *Branding Your Heart*, and I am extremely proud of you. Now, comes the real innovation and upkeep of your brand and its message as you move forward. We, now, need to discuss **content**.

As previously mentioned, everything you communicate with the outside world will be based on your story. As your strategy follows your story, your content will follow your strategy, linking all the way back to your brand's impetus—your story! Throughout the process, you are never to be several steps away from the story that prompted you to begin your work in the first place. However, just because your story is the driving force behind all you do, you must keep everything vibrant and fresh while reminding your audience and "persona" of why you are here, and why they are participating. Nothing does that better than great content.

Content can take on many forms, including video, photos, music, words and more. Of course, each of these you choose to use is completely up to you, but should still be tailored specifically to the persona and group of people to which you are reaching out. If your people are younger, photos, short videos and briefly worded posts might be your best bet, whereas an older group might call for prose the length of newspaper articles. Just know your audience.

Innovative creativity is key in developing great content. The purpose of your content is to engage and create a continuous dialogue with your targeted persona or audience. This content, no matter the type, must be relevant and powerful because each bit of content is meant as a call-to-action your targeted audience should want to obey. This call-to-action in your content must be clear upon sight. Therefore, make sure your content is specific to the form of your chosen social media outlets. Not each outlet is the same. You would not post a hour-long video on Facebook or a 420-character message on Twitter.

Though the development of any content you create would be based specifically on your strategy, chosen social media outlets and target, those three parameters still provide ample room in which you can be breathtakingly creative. I really want to hammer this point home for you. You are completely allowed to creatively step outside the box in order to grasp and keep the attention of your target, as long as you don't lose the heart of your brand.

When it comes to developing prose for your blogs, be as vivid as possible without being offensive. By this time, you know your target and its language. Harness their speech patterns, making your words specific to them and your charge as you also give information that newcomers can pick up and understand. You want your content to be inclusionary and exclusionary at the same time. Your target needs to feel "at home", while your "newbies" need to feel welcome in your playpen.

Pictures are not worth a thousand words. They are worth what your audience deems they are. So, if your photos speak the heart of your story to a ready audience, you need to be prepared for an influx of activity. However, if your photos and memes are turn-offs, you might be the only person admiring a photo out in the middle of nowhere.

Videos, on the other hand, are worth far more than a thousand words. Because they have the ability to weave multiple art forms into one massive collage of ever-evolving information, videos are a go-to tool for anyone desiring to convey information. However, because the society we live in desires things quickly while not wanting to wait half an hour for a meal, it is best your video is entertaining and gets to the point...*fast*. Most people checking their social media feeds during the day are simply not in the mood for a video that eats up their lunch hour and their other two fifteen-minute breaks. Get in. Speak your message while you entertain them. Get out. This is exactly why Vine videos have been so successful in recent years. Within six seconds, you can have your audience cackling with laughter or crying with tears running down their faces. Speak a clear, concise message while holding your target's attention, and watch your people come back for more.

Using only one form of content can get the job done, but I strongly suggest you use a combination of several in order to keep things interesting. No one wants to wake up every morning to read a Shakespearean soliloquy, just like not everyone wants to see the most vibrant video at one in the morning. The times you post, as detailed in your strategy and its analytics, will dictate what *type* of content to post.

Now, there are some of you out there that, even after us discussing the creation of content, either just don't want to bother with it or (clears throat) lack the talent to create it. Read my next words carefully—***that is completely normal. Not everyone is gifted the same way.*** Nevertheless, your completely understandable inability to create content on your own should not be an excuse that prevents you from getting your brand out there. There are plenty of people in your area with the knowhow and energy that will produce and shoot videos and write copy for you! Just ask around and Google what you need. Most, if not all, copy and videos can be written or produced and sent to you via the web. It all comes down to the amount of money you can invest in the development of your project and its content.

To those of you who wish to employ others in the creative development of your content, get ready to be blown away by the level of work others can produce for you. For those of you choosing to self-develop your content, be prepared to be blown away by what *you* can produce. Either way, we are all going to be successful. So, let's loosen our fingers, prepare our cameras, and even find some great music. It's time to create some *awesome* content!

INFOGRAPHICS

There are times you need to convey a large amount of information, and text simply will not do. Though we have the option of photos and videos that we will get to in just a moment, there are times when the combination of text and graphics are the only way to go. There is a word for this wonderful combination: *Infographics*.

As previously stated, infographics combine text with an image in order to concisely and succinctly convey a large amount of information. Infographics can be graphs, maps, timelines, blueprints, or a number of items that combine the simplicity of text with the visuals of images. But, just because these are very useful tools, they should never be abused or used in places that might contribute confusion to a message. When creating infographics for your site, or for posting on your various Social Media platforms, follow these useful tips:

Be Precise

There is nothing worse than seeing a collage of infographics that explain everything no one wants to know about the one thing everyone couldn't care less. Relevance and precision are the orders of the day. If you are going to use this tool, use it correctly by posting **necessary** content that directly conveys the message, emotion, and imagery you want your audience to see. You want your followers to feel enriched and educated when they see your infographics. The worst thing is your followers seeing your infographic and finding no value in it or being confused by it.

Ensure that your content focuses on the message you are trying to convey. In many instances, designers produce complex visuals that get lost within its intended purpose. Make the content as pointed and viewer-friendly as possible for those who will come across your infographic.

Be Innovative

You stand apart from everyone else because no one can be you. If someone imitated you, they couldn't be you quite like how you do it. If your brand must be unique, your content must be unique. If your content must be unique, every infographic you create and use must be unique. Innovation is absolutely necessary simply because you have no clue as to whether or not someone has seen the information you are posting.

What if they not only saw it somewhere else, but you presented it in the very same fashion someone else did? Not only did you not offer anything new, you wasted your viewer's time. This ensures that they almost never see your information or visit your site again. You must prevent this from happening by making sure that you give your followers and visitors something bold, new, and captivating as you present your information.

If you perform a Google search for infographics, you will realize that there are millions of image results, making it increasingly difficult to differentiate your content from others. Your strategy should be varied with font and design styles. Take a look at the following sites to get a better understanding of the look of infographics.

- Canva.com
- Inskape.com
- Gliffy.com

Be Factual

The most imperative component in your infographic creation is making sure you are factual. You content must be accurate and sourced. What is the point of posting inaccurate information? The moment your information is seen as inaccurate, false, or—worse still—untrustworthy, is the moment you must prepare to lose followers. Remember that you are considered an authority on the information that you provide. If your trusted authority can no longer be trusted, there is no use in you continuing to seek them for information.

I would like to add that accuracy is not only necessary for infographics. You must be honest, accurate, and truthful in every aspect of your brand. The moment you are not, everything about you and your brand is called into question. You are a spokesperson for a large group of people that do not have the platform you have. It is imperative that you treat their story and yours with the utmost respect. The moment your brand steps onto the world stage provided by the internet and Social Media is the moment everything you do faces scrutiny, even in the smallest amount.

Therefore, do your best to ensure accuracy and integrity at every stage of your brands development.

GENERATE FUNDS

Now, I want to discuss a few things with you that you should keep in mind as you are developing content. Remember the purpose behind your content. You are creating a language that your brand will use to carry on a continuous dialogue with your audience and your followers. However, no non-profit can exist on content alone. No, my friends. You're going to need some financial assistance to carry on your work in your various field. Therefore, it's time we talk about the main purpose behind your content: **generating funding.**

That's right. I said it. **FUNDING**. I know you're not in this for the money, but you're going to need capital to keep things running, and great content leads to your people opening their hearts *and* their wallets to you. How you go about generating funding is completely up to you because people are forming a connection with *you and your cause*. If they are connected to you, their voluntarily offered donations will follow closely on their heels when you provide excellent calls to action that are filled with passion for the cause.

But, how do you collect these donations? How do you make donating to your cause a safe, quick, and efficient process for your followers and you? There are two methods I use that I'm sure you will find useful in your endeavors. They are SquareCash and Paypal. Both of them are digital financial platforms you can use to easily and quickly collect funds.

SquareCash

SquareCash is genius in that it completely makes the transference of funds a personal thing by linking itself directly to a user's mobile phone. You will quickly see the benefits of it upon downloading their straight-to-the-point app. Once you have it set up, your followers can literally text you their desired donation amount to your organization's mobile phone number, or the mobile number you've chosen to link its debit card. All you must do is "Accept" the donation, and the amount is directly deposited into your organization's account to which the debit card is connected. Plus, most deposits post to your account the same day! If it does not post, the transaction will post within 2 to 3 business days. Your contributors *never* see your debit card information or your bank account number, so your safety is well in hand. For added safety, you can enter a pin number that the app will request anytime a transaction occurs, just in case you lose your phone. Therefore, no one will have access to your financial information. Also, if you want to see a list of donor transactions, simply check your statement via your financial institution's methods.

Download and open the SquareCash app.

1. Open the app, enter your mobile phone number or email address, and tap "Next." A confirmation code will be texted or emailed to you.
2. Enter the code in the app and tap "Next."
3. Add a Visa or MasterCard debit card so you can send and receive money. Enter the card's expiration date, CVV, and billing ZIP code.
4. Select your primary use for Cash. It can be Personal or Business. For our use, choose Business.

5. After selecting Business:
   a. Enter your display name, which will appear publicly to your customers.
   b. Choose a Cashtag – your unique identifier that customers can use to pay you.
   c. Verify your legal name, date of birth, and the last 4 digits of your SSN.

PayPal

The second option through which you can receive funding is PayPal. This digital platform acts as a go-between checkout service. You have likely seen PayPal's icon during the checkout process of your favorite online store. To set up your merchant account, visit the PayPal website.

1. Click "sign up today".
2. Choose premier or business account as the type you want to set up.
3. Choose your country.
4. Click "Continue".
5. Fill in all your information.
6. Click "Continue".

After you set up your account, follow the step-by-step process that PayPal will guide you through to begin receiving funds and processing transactions as a merchant. Like SquareCash, no one will ever see your financial information, so your safety remains intact.

Behind every great cause there is a general line of support that undergirds the mission either through monetary or volunteer contributions. Through compelling storytelling and content, generating revenue can become relatively simple in comparison to how to manage those funds. It is important to choose a payment gateway with low transaction fees that is easy to maintain while providing the user with an experience with minimal steps from the starting point to the donation point. SquareCash and PayPal fit these requirements.

GENERATE an AUDIENCE

We know that the type of content you generate, in a large degree, is based on your brand and the people you want to reach. Yes, you want to reach everyone.

However, connecting to the Internet and going to every Social Media platform without a plan is going to lead to plenty of headaches and questions regarding why your efforts have failed over and over again. You must follow your brand's strategy. Right now, I want you to begin thinking of the type of content you wish to post on Social Media sites, and not just on your website.

The type of content you are going to release to the masses is affected by the Social Media platforms you choose. The type of content you post on Facebook might not necessarily be the same content you post on Twitter or Instagram. You see why I said you need a plan? I'll offer you something about strategy right now: *your strategy is linked directly to the audiences native to the Social Media platforms you choose.* Though Facebook, with its enormous online population, is likely the first platform that comes to your mind when you're thinking about posting online, you will not necessarily find the same audience on Twitter. Different age groups of people with different mindsets flock to the Social Media platforms that best speak to who they are.

Though members of your audience might have a ubiquitous presence online, being present on every Social Media platform ever created, the odds are that a large percentage of your followers will be present on no more than two or three. Though your followers are only on a few, you face the task of choosing the platforms that will provide you with the largest reach into the lives of the people who will follow your brand. This requires a bit of research.

Think about the age, background, career fields, and interests of the *persona* you are trying to reach. That "person" is likely similar to you! Which Social Media sites do you most often visit? On which of those sites are you the most vocal? The answers to both of those questions will also be the answer to the next question: *Which Social Media platforms should I choose?* Though it is the question I am most often asked, it is the easiest question to answer. You begin—and, notice that I said "begin"—with the platforms that you know best, and they are often those you most frequent. If your audience mirrors you, begin with what is easiest for you.

Let's examine some of the most common Social Media platforms, while keeping in mind that your presence throughout each of these platforms should be as similar as possible. From choosing the photos of your pages people will visit on your chosen platforms, to the logos you would use to identify yourself, keep everything about your brand as cohesive as possible from one platform to the next.

Facebook

Facebook, as you should already know, is the largest Social Media platform on the planet. As of the writing of this book, Facebook boasts an online population of 1.393 Billion active users! If Facebook were a country, it would be the second most populated country on the planet. With those numbers, you can attract plenty of followers on this platform, even in the face of many younger users staying exclusively on Twitter and Instagram.

Facebook allows you to post status updates, photos, and videos, but understand that Facebook will allow you to reach only so many people with your posts, particularly if they are funneled to your organization's page through 3rd-party posting . This is not necessarily a bad thing, but it does require you to do some thinking and be strategic in your posts. In order to get started on Facebook, you must create a Business page for your brand. There is a difference between a Business page and a Personal profile, the first being that a Business page can only accept "Followers" and not "Friends". There are other minute details that differentiate the two. However, you will discover those as you further employ your Facebook Business page in your strategy.

To create a Page:

1. Go to facebook.com/pages/create
2. Click to choose a Page category
3. Select a more specific category from the dropdown menu and fill out the required information
4. Click "Get Started" and follow the on-screen instructions

After entering the necessary information to get started, make sure you customize your page and ensure that it carries the look and feel of your brand.

Be unique so that you will gain the attention of future followers, but remain within the "barriers" of your persona. You do not want to be so different that you alienate the people who are most like you. After you are up and running, you can use your Business page to post all the necessary status updates, photos, and videos you choose. Make sure you use a mixture of the three. Not everyone wants to read a post, just like not everyone wants to see videos or search through a list of photos. Keeping a mixture of the three ensures that you reach as many people as possible.

Twitter

Twitter is the Social Media platform where you will find most of the younger generation communicating with one another. Yes, there are others, such as SnapChat, but Twitter is the crossroad where you will see just about anyone you do not see on Facebook and many other platforms. With almost 300 Million active users, you cannot go wrong with Twitter.

Like Facebook, Twitter allows you to "tweet" various updates, but only with a 140-character limit. This is good because most of today's society has a very short attention span. In addition to the text you post, Twitter allows you to record videos on your favorite smart devices and directly upload them to your Twitter feed. The wonderful thing about Twitter's short posts and its video feature is that it can handle the quick posts that come to your mind at a moment's notice. Instead of only reaching the group of people that "Like" your page on Facebook, your posts on Twitter are accessible and visible to everyone on Twitter. Though Twitter might seem like many people yelling in a forest, there is something to be said about the people next to you in the forest passing your message along to others.

Just like you can upload text and videos, Twitter has its own photo feature. So, snap away to keep your followers visually interested in your brand.

Setting up a Business Twitter account is beyond easy.

1. Visit www.twitter.com, click the "Get Started" tab on the right, and fill out the necessary information to complete that step.

2. Choose a unique username that reflects your brand.
3. Select a profile photo, preferably your brand's logo.
4. Create a small bio of 160 characters to tell a concise version of your brand's story and what your brand is about.
5. Include a URL so your followers and others can find you on the web.
6. Create or select a header image that will reflect your brand and its style.
7. You're ready to go! Start tweeting!

Follow any additional instructions to create your page, keeping in mind to be unique in choosing a Twitter handle and the proper visuals for your Twitter page. Like Facebook, there are differences between an individual's Twitter account and a Business account. Remember—I cannot stress this enough—to be unique, but stay within the boundaries of your persona. Do not lose yourself in trying to be so unique that you forfeit the identity of your brand. What people see on Twitter should be as close of an approximation to what they see on Facebook.

Instagram

Instagram, now owned by Facebook, is a unique Social Media platform in the fact that is is photo-based and almost exclusively mobile in nature. Facebook purchased Instagram for $1 billion simply because of the far-reaching nature of photos. Over 30 billion photos have been shared on Instagram, and there is a reason for that. A photo is far more quickly processed by the human brain than text, making a photo more desirable than just a sentence. Cross that with the mobile presence of Instagram and you will see the common sense desire for Facebook to own this platform.

Instagram is brilliant in its simplicity. Millions of photos and 13-second videos uploaded on a daily basis provide an excellent, visual avenue through which a brand can gain an online presence. Where Facebook would function as a hub for all three (text, photo, and video) types of posts, and Twitter being a shorthand version of Facebook, Instagram would be the bastion of shorthand and mobile, visual content in your strategy.

Like Twitter, setting up your Instagram account is a snap. Simply download the app to your mobile device and follow the instructions to create your brand's account.

1. Sign up for an Instagram account, choosing a username that clearly represents your brand.
2. Add a profile photo, a biography, and a link to your website.
3. Link your account to your other Social Media platforms.
4. Announce to your followers that you're on Instagram, letting them know your Instagram username.
5. Use and search tags to connect with your audience.
6. Start sharing photos on Instagram and across your other social networks.

Remember to choose a proper Instagram handle that will identify your brand. This would preferably be the name of your brand, just like you would use on Twitter or Facebook. Remember to mirror as closely as possible everything you can from one platform to the other so your followers and future followers can easily locate you online. After you have completed the necessary steps, snap away and shoot the videos that fit the strategy of your brand.

YouTube

Across the digital engagement world you will hear "content is key". It is, without a shadow of doubt, a very imperative component to your media strategy. As one of the fastest growing social networks with viral content and value to match, YouTube is a great tool for reaching potential advocates and sharing media. In order to sign up for YouTube you must have a Google Email (GMail) account. Signing up for Gmail is absolutely free. First, let's take a look at some of YouTube's features.

YouTube is owned by Google, and this is a wonderful thing for non-profit organizations. Google offers a suite of excellent features for non-profit organizations through AdWords. AdWords (Google Ad Grants) is Google's online advertising tool. Google Ad Grants empowers non-profit organizations, through $10,000 per month in in-kind AdWords advertising, to promote their missions and initiatives on Google search result pages. I cannot explain to you how awesome this is. By following Google's guidelines, your organization can take advantage of a plethora of resources, including YouTube and various Gmail options, that will do more wonders than you can count in taking your brand to another level.

To access these features, begin by creating a Gmail account. Google has made their set-up processes one of the easiest around. As with all Social Media, simply follow Google's step-by-step process to set up your account.

1. Visit www.youtube.com, and sign in using your Google account username and password.
2. Click on your account profile picture to reveal the Google Account Menu, which will also be displayed near the top-right corner of the screen.
3. Click on the "My Channel" link in the upper-right of the screen. The "Create Your YouTube channel" screen will be displayed. Click on the

"Edit" link that's associated with the "From Your Google Profile" option to customize your Google profile.

4. Under the "Activities you'll share on your channel" heading, you'll see four options: "Like a video," "Comment on a video," "Favorite a video," and "Subscribe to a channel." Add a checkmark to the checkbox that's associated with each activity you wish to give your viewers.

5. Click on the "OK, I'm Ready to Continue" button. Your YouTube Channel has now been created. Start shooting and adding videos.

Once you are done, you have access to Google's free suite of tools, including YouTube. However, you must follow the additional guidelines of Google's AdWords to qualify for the extra perks. Trust me. You **WANT** to follow their guidelines. You will not regret it.

Once you are up and running, take advantage of YouTube and shoot the videos that will help increase the reach of your brand. As you develop and upload your videos, create playlists that will seamlessly move your viewers from one video to a similar one. Keep your audience engaged with your video content, and always remember the necessity of brevity. Never allow any of your videos to be longer than necessary. Grab your audience's attention; drop your message in a creative way; and leave your audience and followers wanting more. Not only do you increase your audience's desire for your brand and its content, you prime your followers to share your content.

Speaking of sharing, always give your followers the audience the option to share your posts, no matter the type of content. By doing this, you turn your followers into footsoldiers who get the word out about all that you and your brand are doing.

Periscope

One of the newest emerging options changing the content distribution world is live streaming. Periscope is live streaming social platform that utilizes Twitter for its audience. Sometimes, you need to get a message out there *now*, and Periscope understands that. Partnering with Twitter allows, Periscope allows you to shoot what is happening in your world and stream it live to your followers! So, instead of seeing smaller videos on Instagram or making your follower's wait for you to upload your videos to YouTube, they can be in the moment with you. This adds a completely different level to communicating with your followers than ever before because your audience will feel a sense of camaraderie with you by witnessing what you are seeing as you see it.

Periscope is an iOS app that can be downloaded from the Apple App store. Once you download it to your Apple mobile device, follow Periscope's set-up process to establish your account and link it with your Twitter account.

1. Download the Periscope app from iTunes. As of the writing of this book, Periscope is not available for Android devices, but my guess is that will change soon.
2. Sign in with Twitter. Though it is a standalone app, Twitter and Periscope are a perfect couple.
3. Create a Periscope username. Might I suggest your brand's name?
4. You're ready to go!

Once you are up and running, use the app to your brand's advantage and immerse your followers in your world!

GENERATE AN ONLINE PRESENCE

There is absolutely nothing wrong with laying the foundation of your brand on various Social Media platforms. However, there must be more to your brand than the occasional post people see on Facebook, Twitter, Instagram, or any other platform. Your idea is entirely too large to be limited to the powers that be in the Social Media sphere. Therefore, your brand must branch out and make its presence known throughout the web. It's time to generate and increase your online presence. Let the expansion begin.

Selecting a Domain

Every single website you have ever visited has what is is called a *domain*. A *domain*, or *domain name*, is an identification string that defines a realm of administrative autonomy, authority, or control within the Internet. In simple terms, it is the identifying name of your website, and **domain** names are formed by the rules and procedures of the **Domain** Name System (DNS). Your domain will identify the hub of your brand on the Internet. This is precisely why I mentioned the necessity of making your brand's designs across the web be as synonymous as possible. Everywhere you are on Social Media should be a direct reflection of your domain. Therefore, it is of absolute importance that you select a domain name that reflects the efforts and spirit of your brand. So, as people surf from one Social Media platform to the next, they will easily locate and follow you. Take my domain and Twitter handle as an example:

Domain name: JancynCo.com, Twitter handle: @JancynCo

As you can see, they are not only synonymous. Both, my domain and Twitter handle are the same. Try to do the same with yours.

But, how and where do you obtain a domain name? I already have an answer for you. You have several options at your disposal that will assist you in registering your domain name on the Internet. Check out the following websites and follow their simple instructions to obtain your domain name.

- GoDaddy.com
- NetworkSolutions.com
- WordPress.com
- Zyon.com

Web Hosting

After you choose your domain name, you are going to need someone to *host* your site for you. *Web hosting* is the activity of providing storage space and access for websites. Just in case you are worried, there are plenty of web hosting options out there for you. Simply perform a Google search for web hosting sites and visit their pages to see which one is best for you.

As you select a host, take a minute to think about the amount of space your site will need. Not everyone needs the same amount of space, so make sure you have a plan in mind of how and for what you are going to use your site. If you plan on developing an exhaustive site, calculate the amount of space you will need for that site and, likewise, if you are looking to develop a more streamlined site.

WordPress

WordPress is an online website creation tool, and a blogging and website content management system. Not only can you register your domain name on WordPress, WordPress will host your site for you. WordPress is a simple, straightforward site that anyone can use to create and host their brand's site. It takes most of the heavy lifting out of managing the content of your site.

WordPress began as a blogging site, but has evolved to be used as a full content management system that boasts thousands of widgets and themes that you can use to bring your brand's site to life. In addition to forums and mailing lists you can use, WordPress does a plethora of things that helps you connect and communicate with your brand's followers. As you develop your brand, I urge you to check out WordPress and all they can do for you.

· To better help you in the development of your content, I have pulled some examples you can follow and placed them below. Of course, plagiarizing is completely out of the question. Be comfortable with your own voice. It has gotten you this far, and it will take you even further. Just use these models below as inspiration as you begin to develop your own content or show certain standards to those you have hired to develop it for you.

Case Study 3.1 BuzzFeed

Buzzfeed works! Simply put, it is the digital Michael Jordan in content creation, methodology and distribution. How so? Through their relative virality approach in content. You might think that the extent of *Buzzfeed's* reach lends itself to the comically accurate lists it post but they provide so much more to their desired audience. Incredibly clever videos of everyday encounters we all experience to investigative reports on real time events are all a part of the grand scheme of making something "viral." The proper channel of where and how content should be distributed is a large component of the formula. Real time events will be posted on a micro-blogging site such as Twitter due to its quick form of instant information users will see and simultaneously share because of the trust *Buzzfeed* holds. You want your content to spread at a rapid pace online? Talk about current trending events and interact with the entities who are already doing so.

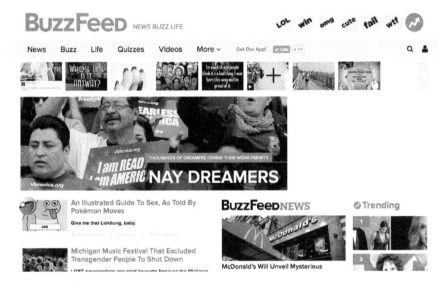

(BuzzFeed)

#PulseCheck: More than likely you utilize Google for all your search needs and never move beyond the first page for your results. This is because those results have high page rankings within Google's super-complexed algorithm for SEO, or *Search*

Engine Optimization. A quick way to get your website or blog post soaring toward page one is to read between the lines. Search for a key phrase within Google and write content based off the results you *don't* see. By doing this you are differentiating your content from the masses and giving it a unique mark that can be quickly identified when people are searching for more specific results.

Chapter 4

The Conversation

The Story. The Strategy. The Content. Each of these is a part of the larger umbrella of something humans engage in everyday. No matter what type of person you are, what you do, or where you live, it is extremely likely you will converse with someone in some way within the next hour. Humanity is a communal species, thriving off of the interaction between its individuals. If we live to communicate with one another in person, there must be some meaning and purpose in us conversing with people around the world. It is either that, or the technology we've developed that allows us to instantly talk with someone in Japan while we're in Germany has no value.

Everything we've discussed up and to this point is all about developing and carrying on an ongoing **conversation** with our target audience or persona. Logging on and using various tools to track the effectiveness of our strategy and content is necessary to see whether or not we are engaging our people in a back-and-forth conversation, not a one-sided lecture. Your plan and mission grows in potency the more you hear from your people about what you've placed out there to get their attention. If you hear nothing from them and the conversational ball isn't bouncing, you are better off standing in a room and yelling at the top of your lungs, hoping for people three addresses down to hear you. If they don't hear you, then you'll have an echo of yourself, at least.

Twitter, Facebook, Vimeo, and all the other platforms you hope to employ flourish not because of a person simply uploading a post, photo, or video. No, they find their value in the answers people provide in response. Once the responses are received, the original poster takes those replies into account when they decide to release the next piece of content necessary to keep the conversation going. This is where you see the fruits of your labor and how your strategy and analytics really shine, because the people begin to relay back to you what they want to see as a result of them viewing the content seed you planted. In other words, for the most part, the people begin doing the "hard work" for you.

Analytics, strategy, and content then come into alignment with the organic outline that actual human beings have provided for you in the seemingly natural conversation that you are carrying on with them. In addition, those same people talking to you will also begin talking to one another. The next logical step to this conversation that once occurred between you and the one persona, is now taking place between you and several other people. And, a group of people communicating with one another and sharing primary similarities on a cluster of views and activities is nothing short of the wonderful phenomenon we all call *community*! This is exactly why you have groups, followers, and friends on just about every single Social Media platform in existence!

There is awesome power in conversation! It builds people up while showing you what binds us all. Our conversations contain certain words and phrases that are indicative of the people with whom we are communicating. The phrases, words, and sentence structures we use in our content shows our people that we are all just alike and that there is nothing wrong with someone in your audience being comfortable in speaking with you. They should feel as if they are talking to "themselves." Who wouldn't love the opportunity to step outside of themselves and converse with themselves? This conversation that you are developing provides people with an experience quite similar to that.

As we speak about developing a conversation, however, I do want to address something with you.

I would like to talk briefly about labels. This little section is going to be a bit heavier than the rest of the book, but I think it's absolutely necessary that we discuss this because we want to avoid any and every trap that will prevent our brands from becoming effective.

No matter where you go in society, each person deals with some sort of label. At times, labels are great because they stem from humanity's desire and *need* to understand and control the environment around them and the circumstances that present themselves in life. However, there are times when labels are detrimental to our personal development and reputation, or even the development and reputation of our brand.

There is a particular word I have often thrown around—one that has placed me in a certain mindset that, though good for several reasons, has shown itself not to be the best word to describe myself or those in my generation. Many of you reading this already know the word of which I speak. However, I will not reveal the word right now because I want to solidify my point before dropping the word on you. Let's take a look at how we define ourselves. In order to do that, we must first go back to our formative years.

The formative years of a human life are comprised of every year between the time of birth and adulthood. There are sections within those 18 to 21 years that are the most crucial. For education, literacy, and a very basic understanding of right and wrong, you would look at years 0 to 6 or 7. To understand how a person perceives the world, the people around them, and how they fit into the grand scheme of things, you would examine the years between the onset of puberty and adulthood. Of course, each of us is still learning. There are people in their fifties still searching for their purpose and how they fit into the world and with people around them. And, the knowledge that we all are still learning adds weight to my forthcoming point.

During our formative years, the beliefs and opinions we have of ourselves, the world around us, the people with whom we have contact, and other things are solidified. Most often, they do not widely vary from the perceptions of our parents or the individuals that have had the greatest effect on our lives. This is the main reason why people believe racism and fear are taught and learned rather than being qualities found in our DNA. The aforementioned solidified beliefs and opinions we have of ourselves are found in the core of who we are. Unfortunately qualities, such as the previously stated fear and racism, find their way into our hearts and become calcified. The only thing, then, that can break up the concrete of the lies we believed in our formative years is the introduction of the truth.

As I stated, this might be heavier than what you expected, but the payoff is coming. Just stick with me as we delve into this subject.

By now, you should be able to see why labels are so dangerous, even on a personal level. There is a collection or set of beliefs we hold in the core of ourselves that affect the perception we have of the rest of the world. Therefore, we believe our interpretation and understanding of the small corner of the vast field we inhabit must be true for the remainder of the field. However truth and labels based on our own limited circumstances is not really truth at all, because truth is true no matter its environment or where it is applied.

After allowing these perceptions to guide us throughout every portion of our lives, we finally arrive at developing our brand, its story, strategy, and everything else necessary for its success. As a result, the experiences or circumstances that heavily contributed to our brand's story have been tainted with the perception and lenses through which we see our everyday life. Believe it or not, people often see our brand and story through our eyes simply because they are trusting us as an authority on the subject for which our brand is touted. Therefore, ask yourself a few questions:

- *Is how I see life affecting how I approach my brand and how others see it?*
- *How have I classified and labeled my brand and its mission?*
- *Does that label support or hinder my brand and its mission?*
- *What changes must I make to ensure I have not negatively affected my brand?*

Remember that your story is a conduit through which others tell their stories. You are a spokesperson for a large group of people with a similar story to yours. Though your story is unique in how you perceive and reveal it and its variables, others find similarities in your uniqueness! As a result, there is a certain level of respect you must give your brand and that your brand must show to others that have either experienced what you have, or have as much of an intimate knowledge of your brand's subject matter as you do.

Everything up and to this point in this section has been about labels in support of me telling you why you should abstain from using a certain 'M' word in the marketing of your brand. You ready for the big reveal? The word you should immediately stop using in the marketing of your brand is...

'Millennial'

Yes, I said it. Having been born in the late 80s and most of my formative years being in the 90s, I can say it with confidence. You read it correctly. There is no use in rereading it, unless you want your jaw to drop again. Now, I already know that a few fellow members of my generation have recoiled in abject horror, while those of older generations are saying, "Finally, someone said it!" Nevertheless, to all of the people in my generation that are thinking of dropping this book right now, allow me to explain why you remove this word from your personal dictionary.

As if the reasoning and logic in the preceding paragraphs were not enough to convince you, I must ask you how many times you have witnessed the use of the 'M' word completely turn off a group of people in an older generation. Think back to the reactions of people you have seen when they read or heard that word. Though members of my generation and I can calmly mention that word around one another, I vehemently suggest the removal of the 'M' word from your vocabulary when you are addressing someone of a different generation. On top of it being the label placed on us as a result of how we approach and see the world, it is an exclusive tag we placed on our foreheads that wrongfully suggests we are the only group within society that understands how the world works or should be ran. That, my friends, simply should not be the case.

Where the label, *Baby Boomer*, speaks of the generation of my parents, my parents did not adopt it as a mark of *identification* like my generation has done with the 'M' word. We have allowed this word to become a method through which people categorize us, and a lens through which people see us. The worse thing about it is that we did it to ourselves! Add to that the fact we are the generation having emerged, or currently graduating, from college while dealing with the horror of the student loan business and the market returning to and surpassing its former glory. All of this is while we are struggling to find careers and jobs that are willing to see things through our eyes and do things our way! We are expecting a world that has seen the emergence and dying off of previous generations to treat us as if we are fresh, new, and the best thing since indoor plumbing, air conditioning, and the Internet.

I know it is frightening to accept, but I will say it anyway: ***The same way previous generations have come and gone is the same way ours arrived and will leave.***

Think about it. No matter the generation, there are aspects of each of them that bleed into latter ones. Each generation has its own way of perceiving and approaching the world. Add to that generation a specific group's ethnicity, socioeconomic level, and their particular faith. With all of these variables interacting with one another in one particular person, how can we rightfully use a word to distinguish ourselves on a macroscopic scale from everyone else when the same variables are affecting each person within the 'M'-word populace on a microscopic scale?

Each and every person on this planet is different. How each person is different when we all share over 90% of the same characteristics in our DNA chain is beyond me. I do not understand how 10% of a DNA sequence can give rise to 7 billion completely different human beings, but I do understand that the only way each of us will survive and live healthy, productive lives is **together**! It is our differences that make this world such a beautiful place. It is our differences that make us so attractive to one another. It is our different perspectives and perceptions of a shared story that makes people get behind our brands and become self-proclaimed champions of our brands' missions. Why, then, would any of us use a word in our marketing strategies and online posts that would put forth even the smallest idea that our brands are specifically for "this" group and not *everyone*?

This is not just for the 'M' word, ladies and gentlemen. This is for any word (within reason) that would give off the feeling that the mission of your brand is specifically for a small group of people and not to be experienced by even the curious web surfer that happened to drop by on your page or saw a smattering of your posts. So, do yourself and everyone else a favor. Avoid the 'M' word, or, for that matter, any segregating word that would produce the faintest feeling of "Us Four and No More!" Simply put, do not corrupt your conversation with inflammatory words.

The developing of a conversation is simple because it's what we humans do all the time. However, that doesn't mean we just hop haphazardly into the process of it. So, let's ask ourselves a few questions about the conversation.

Questions to consider...
- What's the subject of my conversation with the audience?
- Is the audience engaging in the conversation with me and/or one another? Or, are they speaking about something else?
- What is my analysis saying about my audience's responses?

- How do I tailor my responses to positively affect the conversation and push individuals to become even more involved with my cause?

Chapter 5

The Power of 'E'

Throughout the first portion of this book, you've jumped head-first into the Social Media universe with a simple, yet effective, assortment of tools that will serve to help your message and story reach countless individuals. No matter the message, you will find the steps and Social Media instruments useful in every facet of the development of your brand. So far, you've made wonderful strides in creating and telling your **story**. Moving on from there, you created and implemented a **strategy**, based on the story you desired to tell, while arriving at a chosen method of releasing that story to the masses. You could be using **micro-blogging**, **blogging**, or multi-media to reach your desired **persona**. Then, you began creating relevant **content** in the effort to start and sustain a **conversation** with your audience. By doing all of this, you've given your brand the human voice it needs to grab people's attention and interest.

The next step is just as organic and simple as what you've already learned, and it's my goal to ensure that you retain the knowledge you've received this far. Here's how: *Chapters 1 through 4 were preparing you for **The Power of 'E'**!* The Power of 'E' is a simple formula you can use to assist you in remembering everything necessary to help your brand maintain that human voice which will attract even more attention. With all of the information you've acquired, you will **ENGAGE** and **EXPAND** your brand's **EFFECTIVENESS**! It's that simple. As you move forward, if what you plan to do does not engage your audience, expand you brand and increase your brand's effectiveness, you must take a second look at what you are planning to do.

Remember those 7 billion people we talked about earlier? Guess what. Half a billion of those individuals are on Social Media networks and are primed to be exposed to your brand. It's your responsibility to engage them. It's not very complicated, and I will lead you through the process. First, let's define a few terms that you might have already heard if you have previous experience in the Social Media universe.

You can and will refer back to these terms as you progress, so keep them handy.

- **click-through**—the ratio of clicks that an internet advertisement receives to page views of the advertisement.
- **hashtag**—on Social Media sites, this is a word or phrase preceded by a hash or pound sign (#) and used to identify messages on a specific topic.
- **trending topics**—topics being discussed more than others.
- **response rate**—it is the percentage of inbound mentions and replies you've received. Or, for those with a bit more experience, it is the number of inbound mentions of your brand handle that you've responded to, divided by the sum total of all brand mentions (excluding retweets/reposts/shares). This equation gives you the percentage of inbound tweets or posts that you've responded to.
- **insights**—on Facebook, this is information about your particular business page's performance.

- **call-to-action**—an image or line of text that prompts your audience and customers to take action. It is, quite literally, a "call" to take an "action."

Now that we have a few words to work with, let's delve a bit further into them and see what we get and how we can use them to **ENGAGE** your audience.

ENGAGE

Depending on the strategy you take to reach your persona, you might employ the use of internet advertisements. Trust me, you've seen them. Unless you're on a secure website like a .gov or .org, you've seen these ads either pop-up when you visit a page or line the length of both sides of the page. If you have a smart-phone (who doesn't?) you've even seen them in a few of the aps you use. No matter where you've seen an internet ad, these attention grabbers are meant to drive what we call **click-throughs**. It's not just a viewing or sighting of the advertisement that the advertiser wants. They actually want you to *click-through* all the way to their page. After all, no television advertisement works until it gets people in the store. The same with an internet ad. The ad doesn't work until it gets people to visit the page.

Another instrument in the Social Media world that garners people's attention is the all-powerful *hashtag*. A hashtag is a simple word or phrase placed after the "pound sign" (#). You've seen these on Twitter, Facebook, and a slew of other sites. Say, for instance, it's Tuesday and you are heavily into fitness and bettering your body. Anyone in the fitness world who uses Social Media knows that Tuesday is aptly titled "Transformation Tuesday." Be it on Instagram, Twitter, Facebook, or other sites, you would upload your post, photo, or video followed by the hashtag, #TransformationTuesday. By doing this, you've joined a host of other people who are commenting and posting about that same topic. The more people post with that hashtag, the more attention Transformation Tuesday acquires, and this simple subject becomes a *trending topic*. A *trending topic* is a subject being discussed more than others on a particular Social Media site. So, if your hashtag has been used quite frequently, causing a very noticeable uptick in the amount people seeing and discussing your topic, your topic would be considered "trending."

If your topic is trending, you might notice a sizeable amount of people tweeting you and tagging you in their posts. Remember how we discussed all of this is about **engaging** and dialoguing with your audience? Your **response rate** is key in this matter. This is the amount of inbound mentions and replies you have received as a result of your topic gaining attention. Various analytics tools can show you your response rate, though Facebook has a specific tool that will show you the overall performance of your brand's page. That tool is **Insights.** By clicking Insights, Facebook will tell you exactly how your page has been doing.

Though you can use all these tools to track the effectiveness of your brand's page and Social Media campaigns/pushes, there is nothing like a great **call-to-action** to get people moving. A call-to-action is precisely what it sounds like. Great ads culminate with a push for people to do something. Never does an ad simply show and describe a product without driving the audience to purchase the good or service. A call-to-action is the energetic push you use to get people to join your cause, so make it exciting!

EXPAND

No matter the initial scope of your story, or the strategy you've implemented, you should never be content with staying where you are. To go "this far and no further" serves only to stifle your brand from becoming the Social Media phenomenon it has the potential to be. Who sets up a business to only cater to a few people? No one! Everyone wants to excel, and those who say they don't only say that after settling for a certain level as a result of their plan not working. **You are different!** You will do more. You will be greater. You will *expand*!

Everything we have discussed up and to this point is all meant to expand the reach of your brand in the Social Media world. After all, the more you engage with your audience, the more it will grow. The more it grows, the greater your reach into different spheres of influence. This is expansion. It's the essence of every business and non-profit to broaden their reach, and this task is not for the faint of heart.

As you successfully progress beyond your limits, let's examine a few terms you will encounter during the process.

- **Search Engine Optimization**—the process of maximizing the number of visitors to a particular website by ensuring that the site appears high on the list of results returned by a search engine
- **Customer Relationship Management**—the use of Social Media services, techniques and technology to enable organizations to engage with their customers
- **Click Per Rate**—payment given to a Social Media outlet, such as Facebook, to allow your ad to be clicked
- **Impressions**—an advertisement tool on Facebook which is used to tell you how many people are looking at your site
- **Paid Content**—A 3rd-party platform paid to produce posts/tweets for you
- **Organic Content**—self-produced content; the most preferred option, seeing that it comes directly from

you. However, it is often the slowest

- **Facebook Ads**—ads seen on Facebook either in your newsfeed, on the right side column of the page, or on the Facebook log-out page
- **Twitter Ads (organic/paid followers)**—ads seen in the Twitter feed. These ads can be deemed as *promoted tweets, promoted accounts,* and *promoted trends*
- **Instagram Ads**—ads placed on Instagram which normally include a photo or short video

So, you've got a few more terms under your belt that you will encounter in the expansion process. However, you might be asking how they affect you. Let's take a look.

Sometime this week, you've visited a search engine. It could be Google, Bing, Yahoo, Ask or Amazon, but each of them use algorithms to bring up the most popular sites that correspond to your specific search. Have you noticed, though, when you search for something, you usually do not go beyond the fourth page of returned results? As a matter of fact, I'm willing to bet most people do not even make it to the third page. You want your brand to be the on the first page, preferably the first option. Why? Simple! The first option is usually the one people most often choose! This can be accomplished by choosing key search words that will cause the search engine to include your brand or website within the top five links. This process is called **search engine optimization.**

As you continue to grow, you will encounter the necessity of providing customer feedback and addressing issues that customers might have. Instead of the traditional calls customers would normally place, you might have noticed an increased number of people voicing their concerns via Twitter and various other Social Media sites. Most airlines have developed Social Media **customer relationship management** departments to handle customer concerns that are relayed to them in this manner because of the rapidly changing atmosphere of air travel due to delays from weather and other unforeseen causes. Not only are airlines engaging with their customers and handling their issues via Social Media because of the industry's rapid nature, they are doing it because it's effective and that is also makes the customer feel like the corporation takes a personal interest in their satisfaction. So, the next time you find yourself with a customer service issue, try tweeting the company and see the response you get. You will be surprised!

Another way people have pushed and expanded their brands is by using **Facebook ads, Twitter ads**, and **Instagram ads**. Don't you dare say you have not seen a Facebook ad. They line the right side of each person's news feed and, at times, pop-up in the news feed itself as a promoted post. You can easily see who is looking at your site on Facebook by using **Impression**. The same goes for a Twitter ad. These pop-up directly in your Twitter feed. Like Facebook ads, these ads can be *organic* or *paid*. Organic is material produced by you, and paid would be the opposite. Of course, there are also Instagram ads that take advantage of the multimedia aspect that Instagram already has in place. Simply upload your desired photo or video that promotes your brand, and you instantly transform your ads that were once text-only into a medium that sticks in people's minds simply because the human brain processes images twenty times faster than it does text.

Though we have all these tools at our disposal in the hopes of engaging and expanding our brand's with ever increasing effectiveness, the question still remains as to the best means by which to accomplish all of this. That would depend on the strength of the call-to-action you wish to use, or the type of Social Media campaign you desire to run. There are 3 primary types of Social Media campaigns. They are **Awareness**, **Advocacy**, and **Activism**. Which one works best for you? Let's find out.

AWARENESS

Awareness ("Stay Informed") campaigns are driven through awareness while relying heavily on providing information with a softer call to action. Your medium for communication focuses on informing your audience about the cause, as well as other pertinent key points that increase your following. For instance, examine the "Kony 2012" campaign created by Invisible Children. This small, San Diego non-profit created a video that shed light on the Central African warlord, Joseph Kony, who recruited child soldiers to fight. Unfortunately, Kony is still on the loose. Nevertheless, Invisible Children and their tactics are the very definition of an Awareness Campaign.

ADVOCACY

Advocacy ("Join the Movement") campaigns are a more moderately aggressive approach in obtaining and maintaining your online audience. It combines both the informative format of Awareness along with a more pronounced call-to-action that you would normally find in *activism*. Through advocacy, other people would begin spreading the word for you and representing your brand—being an *advocate* for you.

...and, finally, there is...

ACTIVISM

Activism ("Take Action") campaigns are the most direct approach in all the various online movements. When creating a campaign of this nature, the call-to-action is the primary focus with high engagement and influence tactics. There is a precise goal to be obtained with measurable results that can be viewed publicly. This format can be seen as a challenge to your audience to put their money where their mouth is in order for them to join the movement your organization is all about.

Questions to consider...

- How are you engaging your audience?
- Through your engagement, have you noticed any expansion? If not, what do you need to change in order to see it?
- The expansion of your brand is based on its effectiveness. Though you are reaching your target audience and noticing expansion, how can you employ methods like Facebook/Instagram/Twitter ads, Search Engine Optimization, and Paid/Organic Content to increase your brand and strategy's effectiveness?

Chapter 6

The Lightyears...

Despite what many people think, a *lightyear* is a measure of astronomical distance. It is the distance light travels in one year. It's nearly 6 trillion miles! With all that you've learned from reading this book, I want you to know that you will go far. The information contained in this handy Social Media manual can be used and referred back to during the length of your stay in the Social Media universe. Though you can walk away from your Social Media project at any time, I wholeheartedly believe that you will stay. After all, seeing the impact you will make on people will produce a feeling like no other. So, enjoy the trip. Go the distance! Thrive!

Like everything, the art and science of Social Media is a cyclical one. Throughout this book, you've seen the necessity of always referring back to what you've previously done and built. We must always stay in close contact with our story as we execute our plan, examine the feedback, adjust our plan accordingly, and engage in an ongoing conversation with our targeted audience. By now, you're already up and running. However, there is never a problem with streamlining everything. So, let's switch up the language to match your newfound Social Media maturity.

I want you to keep four words in mind: *identify*, *position*, *optimize*, and *analyze.* Each of these words can be used with some of the key words you learned early on in the book. For instance, you learned to **identify** your story and persona. You, then, **position** yourself to implement your chosen plan and strategy. As you execute your plan, you **optimize** it in order for it to perform to the best of its ability. Afterward, you **analyze** the feedback and responses to your strategy. In the same vein in which we've evolved vocabulary to describe the process used to implement a successful Social Media campaign based on your story, that same campaign will evolve as your brand continues to communicate and become more effective and sophisticated in voice and style.

Let's delve a bit further, however.

IDENTIFY

Though you have your story and your brand is expanding, it must have an identity in the Social Media universe. As you have properly pegged your targeted persona, your brand must stand out when your audience is searching for you. In order to increase the likelihood of people landing on your page or hearing about your brand, proper key words must be chosen to identify you online. I *strongly* suggest your chosen keywords fall directly in line with your story, your brand's message, and the emotions and images you want your audience to think of when hearing about your brand. All of this working together increases your overall identity on your chosen Social Media platform. The more distinct your keywords are from your competitors, the more likely you are to be found organically through search engines.

POSITION

Positioning is everything. Take sports as an example. Regardless of the sport you play, the position of your body on the field, the position of your hands on the baseball bat or golf club, or even the position of your fists in a fight will make or break your success in that sport. The same thing goes for Social Media. You must position yourself on the proper Social Media platform that is conducive to your message and targeted audience. If you are doing the right thing, but in the wrong place, you will quickly discover all that your brand is doing is ineffective. Know the Social Media outlets at your disposal. *Choose where your movement will reside online so that your brand will be in the **right** place doing the right thing!*

OPTIMIZE

Optimize and **Identify** will sound similar because of their dependence on key words, but I can assure you they differ because of *where* you are placing those key words. To be properly identified, your key words are selected with the main goal of increasing traffic to your brand. As you optimize, however, those key words are placed *within* your brand, heavily relying on the integration of those words and phrases to connect each of your chosen Social Media networks. You can accomplish this through various titles, descriptive tags, and hashtags for microblogging on Twitter. Whereas you are identified by specific words, these words now serve to optimize your content, thereby making them become synonymous with your brand.

ANALYZE

Up to this point, you've done everything you need to do. Feedback is pouring in. You're getting responses back from more people than you could have imagined. What are you going to do with all this information? **YOU'RE GOING TO STUDY THIS DATA!** I cannot express to you the importance of constantly monitoring your rankings. You must know how people use your site, how they arrived, and the expectations they have of your organization after their contribution. This requires a thorough understanding of your **demographics**, or to whom you're speaking. Remember your persona and targeted audience? Analyzing all this data allows you to make changes when and where necessary to continue the expansion of your brand and ensure its success.

Currently, we are using our laptops and computers to handle most of the heavy-duty work our brand's require us to do. However, we are quickly reaching a point where everything our brands require will be tackled and handled on our mobile devices. Think about it. When the mobile phone was invented, it was an albatross in comparison to the machines that we have now. The only thing you could do was make a call, and that was if the signal was strong enough, you were close enough to a cell tower, and your arm didn't fall off from carrying around the phone's transmission box. Now, transmission towers are cleverly constructed and are everywhere. Are phones are handheld computers that would run rings around the personal computers and laptops of those in the early 2000s. Your smartphone is just that—a brilliant piece of equipment that, amongst millions of other things like snapping photos, recording videos, and hosting video chats, can make phone calls.

Soon—and I mean that with the utmost sense of urgency—we will be able to create and consume content and communicate with anyone anywhere at any time all from the palms of our hands. Who knows? We might even have cerebral interfaces that allow us to do all of this from our brains. Yes, I know that has a sense of *Star Trek* to it. However, we have iPads now, and *Star Trek: TNG* showcased that invention as something belonging exclusively to the 24th century. As you can see, we are several hundred years ahead of what that show predicted.

So, ready your brand. Keep things on the cutting edge, always looking for new, innovative ways to reach and enthrall your audience. As technology continues to shift, we will find ourselves with fewer and fewer limits that prevent us from penetrating markets that were once unknown to us. All that is required of us is to be ready and continue imagining new possibilities.

Questions to consider…

- What keywords are you going to use to better identify your brand?
- Now that you've instituted your plan, on which Social Media platforms have you positioned yourself? What other platforms do you see being used in the future?
- You've used keywords to help identify your brand across the internet, but what words are you using *in* your brand to help optimize it?

- Your brand is receiving feedback, but what are you going to do with your newfound data? How will this data assist you in better targeting your demographics?

...AND BEYOND

By now, your brand is functioning on all cylinders, and that is truly a wonderful thing. Some people have tried to do what you are doing. Where you are succeeding, they have failed. Others have walked away because of the challenges Social Media presents. But, you are still here! I want your brand to thrive and succeed. One day, I want to log on and see all that your brand has accomplished and all the lives it continues to touch. Though you will be presented with some questions and challenges about where to go next, you will be able to face all of them with the wisdom and confidence necessary to stand the test of time.

You're not just sitting down at a computer with a great idea. You've taken on the task and purpose of changing the world. Trust me. It's a fun and rewarding thing. However, I want you to remember something: No matter what brought you to the Social Media universe, or your purpose in developing a voice that will resound throughout the net, your brand must speak of something near and dear to you. Your brand should never deviate from what makes it special, and that, my friend, is **you**! After all, you didn't sit and read this helpful book to merely brand an idea. You've gone beyond that to **Branding The Heart**!

www.ingramcontent.com/pod-product-compliance
Lightning Source LLC
Chambersburg PA
CBHW071223050326
40689CB00011B/2427